CHINESE CULTURE

JIA MAN   WEN JIE

AMERICAN CLASSIC PRESS

AMERICAN CLASSIC PRESS

Published in the United States of America

By AMERICAN CLASSIC PRESS

1178 Broadway

New York

NY 10001 USA

E-mail: us-acp@outlook.com

Visit us at http://www.us-acp.com

Jia Man, Wen Jie

   Chinese Culture

ISBN: 979-8-3304-1533-5

Manufactured in the United States of America

10   9   8   7   6   5   4   3   2   1

CONTENTS

Mirror of Life

With light footsteps, I will ascend the stairway ablaze with flames.

A naked butterfly dances, singing the final verses of life.

The tides of time gently sip from me,

Like ethereal, melancholic music flowing towards you.

Oh, that name, a wanderer of countless years in the world,

Suddenly flashes in the river of your memory.

Dong Xiao[1]

The classical rhythm flows deep into the soul,

Dragging the shadow of moonlight across the sky.

Oh, all the sorrows of the world

Gleam with the luster of snowflakes,

Like a dream, lost in reverie.

The moon hangs over mountains, geese landing on the flat sands.

Barefoot, I wade into my river of night,

As the bells chime in the temple.

An ancient home in the east beckons.

The heart of the flute player is an empty expanse.

Tears of dreams are shattering like shooting stars,

Scattering the fragmented regrets of time.

The gentle sound of the *xiao* weaves an enchanting spell,

Tonight, you and I, from a former life, lift a glass high.

The large wine jug, brimming with bamboo leaves and memories,

Carries lofty aspirations and intoxication.

The inspirational bluebird of the soul gracefully flutters.

A delicate stream of poetry

Flows for a thousand years through the *dong xiao*.

What still shimmers in your clear eyes

---

[1] The *dong xiao*, also known simply as *xiao*, is a wind instrument in the category of aerophones. It is a very common traditional instrument in China.

Are the faint dreams of drifting smoke half a lifetime.

My fallen leaves, in the autumn wind, dance alone.

You are the crystal flow of a murmuring spring.

The kindred spirit of the lofty mountains fades

From grace in mere words;

I graze the white dew's lament of the vast sea.

Echoing back is the endless universe.

In this world, it is too challenging to be stirred.

The *xiao* is jade, the *xiao* is porcelain, the *xiao* is bamboo.

Perhaps it is as deeply eager as we are.

Let it evoke the initial tenderness in every note.

I'm the final chivalric spirit after the *xiao*'s last sound.

In the Name of Rivers

Rivers, in the grip of time's relentless flow,

Disappear into the vast expanse of plateaus.

Wild spirits migrate toward the icy heights.

Mountains stand forlorn, their essence bared to sight.

Both past and future selves, in powerless plight,

Bear witness as grids strain under burdens of might.

Lightning writhes, plundered from waters below.

Ancient mountain streams face a shocking, dire throes.

Waters erode the verdant, sapphire-hued slopes.

Fields yield to the deluge, as hope wanes and copes.

Homelands, generations old, beneath waves now lie.

Dams tower, nightmares wrought, where fish cease to fly.

In caverns deep, a frigid, warning glow emerges.

Whispers caution, forbidding approach.

The last herb, on the bank, gasps for life's breath,

As once untamed rivers submit to man's deft.

Imprisoned waters, breaking resolve with might,

Refuse fate's hand, and its relentless blight.

To whom do we plead, who'll heed the river's plea?

In the name of rivers, who'll set them free?

Scarecrows of Bajia's Village

In Zongke's realm, where rain whispers sharp as needles fall,

Bajia's paths, jagged as tales untold, enthrall.

Fields, untouched by urban sprawl's coveting eye,

Where hues dance freely neath the boundless sky.

Simple fruits are untouched by mankind's tinkering hand.

Birds in dense flocks traverse the heavens' span.

In Bajia's embrace, the scarecrows oft convene,

Divine forms amidst the wild, unseen.

By day, cloaked in rags, they sway with the breeze;

By night, they tease the owls with playful ease.

Never to the county's hub have they strayed,

An umbrella's gift, a bridge to cultures laid.

Scarecrows, chewing seasons' heat and chill,

Exile another's essence in the river's will.

Fireworks

Smoke is the ethereal wings of blossoming flowers,

As tears weave into the drifting souls of sorrow.

Embrace me with hands that raise your toast;

Envelop me in layers of hushed silence.

Your passion ignites my fatal blaze,

Condensing myriad rebellious flowers in its inferno.

In the sepulcher of emotions, we lie dormant,

While brilliant dreams wander through ancient melodies.

Your mood becomes my destined exile;

Your fervor is my tears that cascade in endless stream.

If exile must be,

Let it be on this very night.

Snowflakes cascade from the sky,

Chilling lofty dreams that try to fly.

Thoughts, unbound from the slimness of red beans,

Are captured by the gaze of your resolute heart.

I shall endure the abrasions of my body and roar out,

Splattering against the current with vibrant waves,

Merging into the firmament.

I am the final smile of the green plum.

I am the proud backbone amidst myriad hues.

I am the fervent love that departs for forever numb.

I am the formula etched before beauty fades.

I am the tale post homecoming to the pristine realm.

My Beloved Baby in Dream's Garden

My baby is fostered in the garden of dreams

As a solitary bird on migration's tide.

His hunger is immeasurable in the celestial sky of dreams.

Last night, he greedily suckled on my lotus-like milk.

The baby in the dream is a precious jade,

His smile glistening like a rare gem.

His milk-teeth emit a moon-like radiance.

The baby is a fostered child in my dream.

Rarely do I tread the path to his celestial sphere,

Though I know he's the lone blossom in the star's embrace.

He echoes the ancient *Xiao*'s melody with a blue howl.

Perhaps a future warrior he'll become,

Or a wanderer in the realm of exquisite melodies, forevermore.

I watch as his wings are rending the icy veil.

His naked body trembles in the twilight's desolation.

I enfold in my arms, yet possess him not.

Only my midnight-black hair dances around him.

I press my lips to the soil of dreams,

Seeking the sunlight that might cradle him.

He implores his perplexed mother

To ferry him to the warm mortal realm.

Is there a wait more enduring than that of dreams?

Within the bounds of my slumber, he lingers, enduring.

He pledges to carry his mother's name

Through the spans of his days.

Yet beyond the name, he is adorned with the appellation *Soar.*

Where does the vessel of dreams chart its course?

Yearning, the infant wishes to encounter his kin

Beyond the borders of reverie,

To race together upon the plains of reality.

The Carver of Seals

Please carve a piece of antique silence,

Standing on the bookshelf of time.

Please carve a fragile flake of winter's snow,

Decorating someone else's window frame.

Oh, carver,

Your clear and austere bones are like bamboo fibers.

What you painstakingly carve

Is the marrow of the *Book of Songs* and the elegance of orchids.

The sun is an uninvited solitary lamp for you.

Kua Fu weeps tears for the countless knife scars on your fingers.

Awakened by a night of *Xiao* playing,

Did you dream the frosts and snows of the Tang and Song?

A smiling green plum ignites

The pure and crystal-clear mood for you.

You long to carve a piece of rosy clouds like jade,

And a monument with an upright name for a lifetime.

What supports every resolute bone in your body,

Is the subtle fragrance of poverty and the transparency of character.

Ris Manba Diaolou

No stone lies barren,

No patch of earth feels forlorn,

Ruins bloom as fervent flowers of the past,

Time gasps for breath in wailing whispers.

In the shimmering moonlight,

Ris Manba Diaolou soars with a spirit loftier than mountain ridges,

For love renders it immortal.

Butterfly: The Phantom of the Cliff

Eyes, deep-set, like ancient voids,

Gaze through the corridors of time.

The spine of a dead leaf butterfly

Unfurls like a riverbed of memories.

Silent stones in the verdant river forest hum a muted melody.

Flames twist and soar,

Etching a smile upon the towering cliff's ragged face.

White mist drifts into the hollowed mountain valley.

A ladle of moonlight submerges a dream in an egg-shaped haze.

You stand frozen, a statue of wailing anguish.

Within, a restless slumber whispers the song of desolate hope.

Beside the springs of happiness lies a sea of bitterness.

Who can ensnare the elusive dream phantoms,

Like fleeing fish in the mirage?

A wandering seed skates down slopes of hues;

Gilded fences hold the shadows of old friends, gazing afar.

Life's springs listen to the symphony of stars,

Breaking the silence of time,

Whose quivering fingers release golden wheat-colored wings.

That's a canvas of deep blue, a petal of heart's scent,

A wispy cloud, and a ribbon of dreams.

Held by the sun and the moon,

And plucked with grace words in their slender dance,

The vast expansive years craft an eternal ballet of primary hues.

The serpent-like text twists and turns, echoing my hurried breath.

Wild music crashes in, scattering tears of a solitary journey.

The swirling landscape morphs into mystical visions.

Vivid reds, unfettered greens,

Desperate blues, crumbling silvers,

Push me towards an exposed spotlight.

Tears turn into laughter as I journey through the night.

Trampling the horizon, creating a mirrored expanse,

A melody is woven as delicately as silk and spells,

Consuming the weariness of a lifetime's journey.

The wind's whispers strip the leaves, adrift in a silvery sea.

Starlight drapes like a quilt,

Tenderly cradling the wounded spirit.

Love of an elusive warmth fleets like a night owl's flight.

Dry grass and chilling stars stir the graves in the depths of the dark night.

The colorful butterfly flutters amid the enchanting notes;

Sandalwood limbs carry the essence of the seasonal scents.

Your gaze, a glistening shard of ice,

Softly meandering, quells my fiery desires.

Twirling in the labyrinth of uncertainty,

It breaks the icy sword of celestial tendrils.

There exists in this world a bond of kinship;

Closer it brings me, scorching me with ardor.

Further it drifts, encasing me in an icy embrace.

In this realm, a whisper of forgetfulness should exist,

Mending the shattered wounds with sublime swiftness.

A rainbow-like butterfly unfurls in vibrant hues.

Its silence and serenity are akin to Zen's beauty.

If the wide sky is her platform for flight,

The boundless sea is a mere backdrop

For her gentle, fleeting silhouette.

The Murmur of Smoke and Flame

The matchbox's slumber awakens with a gentle touch.

It yearns for smoke flickering in restless eyes.

Sparks fuse wood into molten whispers,

As wood sighs the whisper of water.

Time dampens the fervor of gunpowder.

Three fingers gracefully ward off the onslaught of wind.

The remaining two fingers tenderly

Ignite memories lost in the shadows.

I hear the echoes of a shattered moon in the sky,

While laughter "chirps", like silver bells, a cascade of joy.

A tree branch heavy with ripe fruits, exuding delight,

Burns fiercely like a rapid-fire serpent.

Tonight, the destiny of a match

Is consumed by its intense craving for smoke.

Its mission is not a tragic play, but a dance of flames.

My imagination wanders through realms of legend.

A wispy trail of smoke intertwines with my elusive thoughts.

Should the match seek escape?

It must either rise like smoke

Or be drenched in the depths of dampness,

Entwined with fate, forevermore.

The initial choice is a dance with destiny,
As the swollen head ignites with the plea of gunpowder.

Who steals a matchstick's quest for forest's breath?
Why does the firelight shun the depth of ebony?
Why isn't it a black stone?
Why isn't it a moon's silvery gleam,
Nor the soft touch of snow in tranquil dream?
When the flame, proud and tall, lifts its head,
A lone cigarette burns into
A pillar to mourn the brightness of the past.

The demise of a pack of cigarettes always starts
With the first flicker of flame.
The withering of a relationship always fractures
After the first seeds of doubt are sown.
Matches, steadfast, never yearn for
The fleeting charm of disposable lighters' turn.
Apathy is the accumulation of prolonged familiarity,
Sucking the sweetness of the past.
Sweetness wanders through the scars of the seasons.
Matches ignite you while you ignite thoughts.
Yet, thoughts give all the pain to powerless, resisting words.
It's a form of aggression.
You bid love to reside deep within the quiet shrine of the soul,
For in mundane expressions, innocence finds divine solace.

In the embrace of autumn's nocturnal sighs,

Cigarettes and flames share whispered lullabies.

A packet of smoke scatters into gray-white dust,

From ardor's chase, both pain and injury.

How bleakly life ages, unlit and alone,

Devoid of flames that once brightly shone.

As the computer in the study lists and sways,

I'm lost in a drunken haze, where words blaze.

With the poet's keystrokes, I fervently write.

Some voices cut through the air,

As sharp as a Tibetan Mastiff's roar.

Please send an email to the grasslands.

Yet I trust your vows shall bend in the dreams of tonight.

Upon this cigarette's end, who shall forsake smoking?

Trust in you, who can renounce the smoke,

To forsake that chapter of love.

The Power of Water and the Nature of Tea

A cup of water's expanse,

And a cup of tea's rich essence,

Offer a crystalline space.

I am the verdant-touched plume,

Where azure streams transform to dew's sweet dance.

The green tail is in the whirlpool of the rapids.

A glance of it

Wanders out of the valley of emotions.

May I reclaim the dream's inception?

Within Lu Yu's grasp,

The Classic of Tea imbues the bygone with rustic charm.

For a millennium, poetic cadences ebb and flow,

Nourishing the exultation and melancholy of countless scribes.

And you, in this present existence,

Your slender fingers grind to dust the dreams.

I cradle upon the verdant windswept pillow.

Please hold a cup of water,

Where verdant peaks and flowing rivers unfurl,

In the vast expanse of your soul.

Please grasp a cup of water,

Where whispers of snow-kissed ponds dance

Within the wellspring of inspiration's trance.

Time is as a vintage wine,

While solitude is as a melody profound.

The cup is a mirror reflecting duality unbound,

Within which your spirit roams, unchained, untamed,

Refusing the sight of waning plum blossoms,

Whose essence reclaimed.

You refuse the vanishing act of gallant shadows,

On the stage of rivers and realms.

A cup of tea's potency mirrors the solitude of a dragon,

Within which the grand river of the heart ebbs and flows in its honor.

Life serves as your paramount vessel;

A tapestry of values shapes the richness of this existence.

Time in a Scoop

Alone I stand, by the stream of autumn's sigh,

Cupping in my palm a mere scoop of time's translucent sky.

Who whispers soft here, in symphony's refrain?

'Tis the patter of rain, the moon's celestial chain.

Enveloped in arms of fiery hue, I gently sway,

Lost in the chromatic woodland's play.

The trees that long to bloom have already begun the graceful dance

in full bloom;

Now their petals dance and fade.

Those craved fruition;

Now their bounty's already displayed.

After storing fervor for so long,

A vibrant world ignites in song.

A lone leaf dreams of solitary roam,

Two in embrace, in winter's gentle home.

Three or five in clusters unfurl their wings of verse,

Transforming into dead leaf butterflies, a poetic whirl.

In the heavens above, like a proud bird we soar,

Chasing the lightning's speed, to be eagles once more.

My memories wander through the boundless forest,

Where the mature, dense canopy conceals a profound chill.

I prefer to lose myself in the vivid canvas of late autumn,

With hands cradling the essence of passing time.

My eyes are akin to the dawn's first light on a crescent moon,

Whose gentle fingers caress the sky's crystal blue ice.

Too many unanswered loves have left me weary.

Shall I mend your fractured spirit with threads of ice

Or offer you a vessel of desolate hope

To gather and heal your wounded soul?

The purple Han Character grows silently

Within the crystal bottle of time.

The crumpled map breathes the moon beyond the Great Wall.

My soar throat rasps like a winter breeze

In the echo of a lifetime.

Amidst the winter snow's soft embrace,

I spy strands of silver in my hair.

Silence witnesses years misspent;

A soul is burdened with regrets.

Time, a handful of flowers, once for me, is in full bloom.

Time, a handful of water, soothes the fervor of my youth.

Time, a handful of sand, caresses the soles of my feet.

How many years reside in that handful of time,

As swiftly as the river's flow,

Washing away the cradle of countless sleepless nights?

The Blossom of Ailment

A flower tainted with illness

Savors the tender fervor of roots and leaves,

With a heart fluttering in agony, a pain that lingers.

In a slumber shrouded in heaviness,

The passageway of veins is unlocked.

Each drop, icy and numbing, in the translucent tubes,

Like a ladle of moonlight pouring the chilled radiance of the sky,

Pours into my vessel.

A flower tainted with illness,

Ingests the essence of Chinese Pharmacopoeia.

Each moment stretching into eternity

Sucks away my confidence.

I heard the sound of blood blending with medicine.

I see the competition for inner and outer life.

The bloody fighting,

In the midst of a spiritual war struggles to rise,

A wager made with illness, a fierce battle cry.

No fear is to be found, only courage and might,

In the wearied days when I feel exhausted.

Family, you are always the first to draw near,

In every moment of doubt and every tear.

A Summer of Solitude

A summer's tale of solitude unfolds.

You departed swiftly, like a mountain bold.

Now the hills are gone, the waters still;

Birds hush their songs, my heart in turmoil to fill.

Lost within my soul, you are a forest unknown,

Where emotions roam free, in the night alone.

Left forsaken in this wild expanse of words,

I stand in solitude, a lone watchman in a world absurd.

In the stillness of time, clamor tiptoes through my threshold.

Do the heavens weep in this elusive season?

Closed tears cascade in a flood of emotions.

A photograph, black and white, stretches like a solitary vine,

Capturing the essence of your fleeting feast in this lifetime.

In this world, a forgotten art known as longing whispers its name.

In the marshlands of memory, melancholy flames are flickering.

I ascend the vessel of bygone days,

To chance upon the tender smile that graces your entire existence.

In the valley deep within my dreams, I whisper your name.

Your form is bathed in moonlight.

Please echo back, those years torn by thorns.

Your hands tell tales of mysteries unborn.

Through storms and tempests, I find my way.

The tunnel of my heart, slowly does sway.

Enchanted by your summer's fiery waves,

Water and fire in a dance saves.

In a solitaire summer, you're the spring that led to my disgrace;

In a solitaire summer, you're the leaf that drifted from my embrace.

In a solitaire summer, the scorching sun forgets to dance;

In a solitaire summer, once-blooming blooms no longer have a chance.

Memories of ice melt,

Drifting towards the distant azure trance.

Chinese Medicine

In the eyes of dawn and dusk I see

The full moon and lunar eclipse in my sea.

Thunder and lightning streak across the land,

Branding a nation with the mark of suffering.

Through five thousand years of splendor and struggle,

Heat and humidity, illnesses and viruses,

They madly dance in the veins.

A crimson plum blossom resides in my heart,

Coughing, coughing, like a melancholic sunset.

Aching soul weeps silently under the night's pre-dawn

Voiceless, yet resounding in the realm of poetic imagination.

In the dawning of a new century,

A sage from Hunan arose gracefully.

He crafted a tonic to mend the land.

Guided by the courage of a nation,

And infused with fiery passion,

All are boiling in the crucible of history.

The mighty Yangtze River endures, whose spirit never yields,

The Yellow River roars, in heart with fury fields.

The healing elixir flows through the earth's trials,

As the flame burns brightly in Chinese hearts.

Stand tall,

For a New China emerges.

In the moon's soft glow,

China's poetry unravels,

Where medicine names whisper of ethereal realms.

Lingzhi, Clove, Yuzhu, Fairy in delight,

Are in a graceful dance beneath the starry night.

Brahmi, Forget-me-not, Pedicularis, Fruit divine,

Their essence ethereal, refined is their spirit.

Ligustrum fruit, Trichosanthes, and Cassia seeds,

Each is graceful, versatile, skilled in both art and deeds.

In Chinese martial arts, a divine connection exists.

A solitary mugwort sprig steps over frost, leaving a delicate trace.

When a wanderer's footsteps mark the path back home,

His mother's understanding heart won't need to roam.

Like a boat of dreams on the water's gleam,

Potamogetons weave a tapestry of a poet's dream.

In the realm of Chinese herbs, where bitterness reigns,

Let them bear witness to history's gains—

Gentiana lutea, Viburnum opulus,

Andrographis paniculata and Pseudostellaria heterophylla.

Whispers of glory and sorrow carry the same.

Whichever emperor reigns above,

Chased the fabled Elixir of Ages?

Who grasps at eternity, in life's eternal test?

Eternal is the spirit of a nation that thrives,

In the endless pursuit of life's boundless highs.

A lone ice chip rests on tongue's embrace.

Upon the icy rock we sit in tranquil grace.

Touching hearts, we could feel the pain,

As a blade of grass sprouts in the worm's vein.

Oh, the agony it must endure,

For the wild diggers in their manic allure.

With a raised pointed hoe so tall,

It scorches the steadfast bones of the snowy mountain.

Green grasses spread as a vast sea;

Sorrowful flora stands isolated, marked by a mournful fountain.

The quintessence of the Chinese medicine tome,

Returns to its roots in foreign attire.

The lofty price of modern packaging cuts to the bone.

The final guardians of the land,

Labor on in the old apothecary's den,

Where their craft is never end.

Dust quietly alights upon the cicada's cast-off shell;

Emerald bamboo splinters adorn the centipede's back.

The formula of medicine is an art, a tapestry of ever-changing hues,

Where medicine restrains and nourishes in mystical dance.

A dainty copper scale,

Weighs meticulously,

Measuring the wisdom of doctors across the lands.

An ancient scent of sandalwood in the air,

Weighs up the burdens borne by every soul.

My heart trembles in awe.

If a strand of fair hair is needed for a dose of medicine,

The smell of chemical despair remains in the bleached tresses.

Should verdant hills lose their hue divine,

And crystal waters dim, no longer pristine,

The ancient elixir of medicine should fade,

Lost to the relentless march of progress.

Treasuring the silence contained in traditional Chinese medicine,
Cherishing the longing for light in traditional Chinese medicine,
We embrace the essence of our true selves as we cherish the
timeless gift of Chinese medicine.

Blue DNA

The long night serenades with a lyrical river,

Within bark-bound family tree.

Dreams tenderly embrace me.

Sunlight cascades over my fingertips with ancient haste,

The new moon's seductive allure from my eyes, gently displaced.

A silent family tree is a forest in distress.

Tears fall in loneliness, the pen's tip gleaming with duress.

The ignorant lineage, understanding denied,

A genetic chain dances with love and anguish intertwined.

A shooting star, like a dreamer's vessel,

Carries the essence of my past lifetime's tears.

Forgive me!

I pay no heed,

To the ancestors' graves in the shadows of night's creed.

The enigmatic dance of *fengshui* is like a web spun,

Resembling the heartbeat of silk, under the sun.

Believe in me!

It is not blasphemy;

An ode to the departed is veiled in mystery.

I would rather believe that my ancestors locked their wisdom

Into the genetic code I inherited.

I often feel that the resilience in my soul

Is a tree sprinting through the jungle.

Legend has it that my ancestors had two generations,
With exquisite gem-cutting skills in their possession.
Their inspiration built a palace of white jade back then.
A lightning struck one night.
Their ancestors from even earlier collapsed into ancient symbols:
"Escape, go far away,
Settle in the lush grasslands, healing a family's wounds."
Ancestors avoided the fate of burial with kings,
A genetic chain constantly bearing fruits in undulating fields.

Forever lost in family ties' intricate web of intermarriage,
Each ecstatic revelation is a winding maze.
Through genetic mountains, riverbed of kinship, I walk.
The weary scholar, lifting his cup in despair,
Sees his lifelong unfilled dreams crumpled and torn.
Unappreciated, it's a life's jagged fracture.
In sorrow's legacy, he finds his roots entwined.
Bitter inheritance distills within my soul.

DNA is an encrypted codex etched in celestial lore;
DNA is a regal azure flame, our human story's core.
In whose veins did the first winding path go through?
Echoes of primordial quirks are like ancient oceans rise.
A tempestuous soul is a personality's surge.

The vast forehead is a canvas where destinies converge.

A ladder of time, a wooden helix unspins,

Guides me through ages, to kin with countless great-grandparents.

Is matriarchal grace, a nurturing strength profound

Or patriarchal roots, in war's ceaseless ground?

Through smoky echoes of a thousand fights,

Boundaries blurred, by history's relentless light.

Was my great grandmother a farmer's wife,

For her hands were stained with earth?

Or was my great grandfather a wanderer's exile,

For his spirit was born of rebirth?

Our blood is a tapestry of vanished tribes' cries,

Each threading a sorrow, lost but woven in my eyes.

The blue DNA, our genetic code silently ties us

To the unfathomable realms

Where the vessels of existence once navigated

Through veils of mystery.

Now, the vast expanse of our future

Awaits the endless journey of discovery.

The genes of wisdom, like celestial lanterns,

Illuminate the depths of the universe,

Yet their profound knowledge can also spark

The fiery warning of catastrophe

If not handled with utmost care.

To the Mountain God

To the ancient sacrificial ceremony for the *Qiang* ethnic group

Amidst the grayish mountains you stand,

Atop the white stone pagoda you sit grand.

In the lush forest, you quietly reside,

Mountain god, please return to your revered side.

On this festival day,

We offer our sincere hearts in pure delight.

Through spiritual dance, our deepest love we impart,

Like a mighty river, flowing from the heart.

From worship a thousand years old,

To this very day, our reverence untold,

Offering plump cows and sheep so true,

Presents fragrant barley wine to you.

May your presence remain forevermore,

In the mountains, forest and river's roar.

In monkey-skinned hat, I am *Shibi* —

Whose memories before life lost to the abyss.

All things fade like snow in the endless sky;

My staff is adorned with golden sun's wrinkles.

Curved fingers point to valleys brown.

High plateau's desolate annual rings

Resemble withered vines of old days,

Twitching upon the bar, burning chains.

Scorching, scorching, into branches of desire,

Dancing, dancing, upon the rugged cliff so dire.

Ancient scripture is the needlepoint of incantation.

Spiritual instrument is a hoarse throat.

To the rhythmic beat of raindrops on the sheepskin drum,

My feet strike the beat, with thunderous grace.

Stepping on lightning and snow under a clear sky,

I reach the solemn gateway to the divine space.

Casting my fiery fingertips towards the white stone,

Consciousness takes flight on untold wings.

I bridge human desires with the will of the mountain gods.

Hey! Hey!! Hey!!!

Amidst the pure white clouds,

On the summit of sacred snow-capped peaks,

Lies the fairyland of the mountain god's abode,

A path where *Shibi* toils, a lifelong feat.

In the realm of day, the sun marches,

While the moon lies in wait in the night's embrace.

Yin lies to the left, *yang* to the right.

Women reside on the outskirts of time, serene and still.

Men at the heart of time are performing a dance of simulated war.

Brave warriors bare their sculpted, naked arms.

Men of wisdom, men of wounds, and men of strength,

You lead and I follow,

Raising clubs, wielding knives, dancing with swords,

Forming an eternal circle, tracing the ancient script dance first.

This is the winding path of ancestral migration,

Wrought with twists and turns.

This is the chest scarred by the pains of war.

This is the dance where the divine bestows vigor

Upon the *Qiang* people,

Etching the memories of battles lost.

Oh, mountain god!

Please bless upon these bare souls!

The sincere heart, the only true deity of this earth,

In fragrant boughs and tender hands of April's birth,

Flows the devout blood of a faithful devotion,

Merged with your supreme being in holy emotion.

In the *Qiang* fortress, the fire burns bright.

An eternal flame never dims its light.

Prayers praise *Erma*'s prosperity and grace,

Beneath the mountain god's benevolent face.

May the mountain god bless the wise and true.

Immortal souls offer tribute anew,

For in humble gratitude, we find our way,

A language of love, nature and the divine sway.

Snow Burning

What melody can I dedicate to thee?

My voice is a wind-pierced disc.

The well of memory swells with lotus light.

Thy pen sketches me in white with gentle might.

Whose life is bound to burn in snow divine?

With tears and mist-filled valleys, it shines.

Sunrise and sunset upon the skyline stand;

Their deep and wistful gaze is love's command,

Silently longing for each other, no regrets in all of time.

The speed of a life ablaze is more splendorous and prime

Than any meteor's fleeting glow on high.

Oh, the beauty, like snow, ignites the sky.

Father's Black Umbrella

Father, what hue does your soul exude?

Why dwell in that realm afar,

Yet drift into my dreams often?

Father, what form does your soul possess?

Why appear to me serpentine,

Coiling in your prior home's distress?

Last night, were you taken by illness?

I beheld you adorned in a robe of sapphire

By intravenous infusion with blue liquid.

A glacial scorn in your eyes

Arouses the flight of passing shooting stars.

Have you taken up the black umbrella anew,

Racing through the shattered moonlit wasteland,

Once again ensnared by memories of a former existence?

People say that death is but another form of birth.

Have you pursued a century of rebellion on this earth?

Does true love stir a heart so unmoved

Or is it time that abandons, flying too swiftly, unwilling?

Is it the weariness of longing, forever alone and frail,

That leaves us powerless, lost in an eternal, endless tale?

Strolling beneath the night's umbrella,

You breathe in the fabric's humble.

Enveloped by love's layers, spanning a lifetime,

Why not surrender in the fire's enchanting prime,

And burn to ashes in passion's wild, blazing flight.

In a seamless dream, I saw you dwell

Next door to hell, your eyes a fiery spell,

With passion's fervor, rolling within,

In sorrow's depths, a crimson flame, akin.

Father, your umbrella is made of bone and soul

Forever caught in a web of torn emotions.

If worldly love could bring about true clarity,

Then it is surely not the enchantment of genuine love.

Father, why in dreams do you call

Revealing mysteries, in love's eternal thrall?

A Date with Flowery Lake:
To my friend ZXC from afar

In the mystical landscapes of *Ruoergai* lies an auspicious sea
Known as the enchanting "flowery lake",
Where the mesmerizing sapphire mirror challenges the heavens every night.
Graceful waterfowl glide over its ethereal surface,
Creating a dreamlike lake in flight.
Legend says within the crystal palace of the "flowery lake",
Dwells a princess of unparalleled beauty as morning's first wake.
Her eyes twinkle like the stars in the night;
Her nose, a moonlit cliff, noble and cold as ice, stands proudly glistening in the icy embrace of the moonlight.

Cuo Cuo, the enchanting princess fair,
Her ethereal beauty is veiled in misty air.
Gracefully she glides on the meadow's green,
Her coral-hued gown a sight to be seen.
Her laughter, a melody of silvery streams,
Awakens the secret enchantment deep within the snowy peaks,
Echoes of mystic lore,
Bidding all to enthrall.

The princess, a wild lightening streak across the prairie sky,

Gazing up at her reveals the Milky Way's branches spread high.

Her beauty is profound and vivid;

Her beauty is in the quiet solitude.

She dances with the winds and the dew,

Her every step a poetic rendezvous.

In a past existence, I was an ethereal azure bird,

Entwined a thousand eons by her side.

Our flight was a symphony against the pristine azure skies,

Where icy streams sparkled like sapphires.

When my wings were ignited by a falling star,

Jade-hued feathers fell away in despair from afar.

Amidst the celestial glow, I saw her forsaken glance

A sorrowful gaze from a distance.

Golden prayer flags dry the tears from her wrist-bound beads;

Their sacred six-syllable chants slip through her fingers' creeds.

I descended into the palace where she rests,

A thousand blossoms unfolded, my love confessed.

Beneath rippling waters, I felt her gentle breath so near,

Blooming into flowers that adorned the highland lakes, crystal
clear.

As she was serenaded by a melancholic symphony beneath the
waves,

The reverent water spirits moved in a flora grace,

To enshrine her delicate essence within Buddha's embrace.

In this lifetime, I have a rendezvous with "flowery lake".

Traversing miles through dust and fatigue,

The sea's transparency whispers of her eons-old longing,

Golden flowers submerged in water, lanterns softly glowing.

I journey with firefly's light,

Seeking the princess from another life.

Grasses stretch, skies ripple, love's quest is devout.

Eagle,please tell me where she sings me the melody of her life's song.

Snow lotus, please lead me to where our beautiful encounter might belong.

The maiden, on a steed as white as morning's grace,

Gallops toward me,

Her beauty, timeless, radiant as the rainbow's glow.

My visage flushes, my heart's rhythm like a drum's echo.

Yet in her eyes, she failed to reflect the "me" that lived a thousand years before.

How can the vibrant butterflies of the highlands

Unveil the river of her memories?

I was her joyous solace in a bygone age.

She represents the happiness I seek in this present existence's final stage.

Blooming April Flowers

I find the transparency of the sky in the sunshine after rain.

The greenery, adorned with a glistening sheen of dew,

Envelops my heart in an eternal dance.

April's shadow, a lingering echo of your absence,

Echos through the petals of the once-flouring peach.

Now, their essence is a testament to poetic grace.

In this enchanting dawn of spring, all is held in thrall.

Heaven's veils flow with a grace that drips and falls.

Birds flit and frolic, flying high and low.

And then I behold you, gliding gracefully where the river glows.

You bite the wild peach blooms with your red lips.

Your soul takes flight.

No weight or chain can bind you from this boundless flight.

Who among us could resist such a captivating sight?

In *Wenchuan*, on a verdant clay mountain, dwells a rustic household,

Where April's allure beckons poets who've slumbered long and cold.

In the fervor of their meeting, they clasp hands in fervent joy,

Their spirit's high, amidst the swirling dust of journeys past.

Brother Long spins tales akin to aged, aromatic wine.

The pleasantness of spring blooms within his finely honed gaze.
Even the trees leaning against the wall strain to catch every word.

Brother Niu is slightly intoxicated.
His beguiling eyes are half-lidded,
Swaying the wisdom shimmering like starlight.
Shepherd-boy Yang diligently attends a steward of fervor.
Zhang Li's language pulls the bow of his style.
Qingjiu and Chenglin are quiet in their shyness.
Trouble-stirring LeiZi provokes the endearing Zeng Xiaoping.
Loquacious Zhou Zheng raises his glass, headless of sobriety.
All are men of great passions, as it turns out.
Meng Fei and Meng Bi nod and sip, offering astonishing insights
that bind, occasionally.

Tow journalists from the TV station have come,
Turning this literary gathering into breaking news.
Scenes of beauty or ugliness in news hold no significance,
For the true beauty lies in the intense aroma of friendship ablaze in
this April.

In the blossoming April,
My weary thoughts yearn for a rebirth,
Confronting the wandering winds and flickering shadows of time.
Silence becomes my sole dialect,
And a speechless void fills my voids.

In the subtle outlines of April,

Countless yearnings and reunions drift away.

Upon the carousel of ages, the verdant earth does fade,

Into dust and sludge, its beauty decaying.

Slowly it slopes towards yonder horizon,

Mimicking the tides of time, a poignant vision.

A group of trees, reaching for their dreams, stand united.

Another cluster, harboring silent desires, whispers in the night.

In the veins of the ancient *Qiang* people's descendants,

How much of their galloping, sorrow-filled dreams still swirl

green?

In the spring rendezvous of 2005,

Life brimming with emotions, what stirs in the *Qiang* bloodline?

Ideas clash with thoughts, like wild storms in the spring rain.

Does the spring breeze mock me, or do we mock the mud of spring?

Spring predates us all.

Do we envy her eternal, youthful heart?

The word "spring" exudes a grace.

Spring's touch softens the icy core within.

As *Qingming* passes, the sky reveals a moonlit night.

April's time-bound wings carry a flower's silhouette into my heart.

Adorned with blossoms, April whispers the language of flowers,

Where the romance of lifetimes resides in the depths of dreams.

An Old House

Behind the bustling Red Pillar Head, the old house sits in desolation.

Its foundation touches the moistened earth, a witness to time's erosion.

The river, swollen by memories of childhood, nearly swept away the delicate soil.

The dwelling leans against the riverside, its three rooms swaying alongside.

Like the wobbly shadow of my childhood,

The gray rubble reflects a solitary despair.

The old house serves as a testament to a vibrant community's past.

Nested snugly within a narrow lane are over thirty households.

Woven wicker fences delineate spaces between homes,

While smoke and flame dance within the open walls, creating an ethereal mist.

A thick layer of dust, akin to a velvety silk, clings to every touch,

Encapsulating the essence of the neighbourhood.

The sound of parental reprimands at one end harmonizes with the light banter at the other.

A communal washboard in the courtyard,

Is worn smooth with shared labor.

Mothers immerse in the chore of weekend laundry,

Their hands lost in soapy suds.
Fathers are absorbed in splitting firewood,
Their strength echoing in each strike.
A majestic walnut tree,
Its verdant canopy is a vast, protective shelter.
Gathering beneath its boughs, children playfully chase and dance,
Ensconced within the embrace of a dream.

I often reminisce about the chaotic funeral
I attended at the tender age of three,
And the throng, a sea of faces, nearly burst through the seams of
the old house.
My grandfather lay still as stone on a wooden stretcher,
His limbs tightly bound, biscuits neatly tied around to his wrist, a
feast for eyes.
Drawn by hunger's allure, I loosed the rope and savored the
forbidden feast,
While the wails of my sister, echoing from that year, still resonate
in the eastern skies.
Carrying a laden basket, my grandfather once peddled his wares
with care, But now, he rests in the majestic mountain's embrace,
forever.

In the old house where we resided for a dozen years gone by,
Like a pocket with frayed seams, this weathered dwelling ages in
the blink of an eye.

Summer's golden rays would frolic upon my drowsy eyes.

Autumn's showers would drum upon our modest abode.

Porcelain, wood, and copper vessels vied to outshine and uphold.

The symphony of water droplets, like a fragile refrain,

Whispered captivating tunes, liberating our minds from the mundane routine.

As dusk descended and our parents ventured away,

To gatherings and films, leaving us to wander and play.

Beneath the gentle glow of an oil lamp's wavering light,

I wove tales of wonder, conjuring shadows in the still of the night.

Imagination took flight as I fashioned stories of mystical realms.

Their unheard whispers guide us with magical helms.

Enveloped in slumber, serenaded by *the Min River*'s sweet song,

We envisioned rivers flowing, graceful and enduring all along.

In the year of 1986, our dwelling soared high,

A five-story edifice against the sky.

Yet *Wenchuan* County felt nature's furious ire,

As floodwaters engulfed the entire town.

Against the tide's wrath, I ventured with might,

To salvage remnants of our cherished sight.

Amidst the soaked chambers, I beheld afloat,

Wandering wooden relics, lost and remote.

As I trod upon a rusted nail's cruel sting,

Scarring my flesh, injustice it did bring.

My parents, their toil, a life's work in vain,

Found only defeat where success should have reigned.

Whispers spoke of our home's former prime,

Eight rooms adorned, a coveted shrine.

In those distant days, when locust flowers breathed,

A mere babe I was, innocence unsheathed.

Within those aged walls, a snake uncoiled,

Watching intently, its secrets never foiled.

Masked workers passed, spreading asphalt's slick sheen,

Quietly crafted roads, their duties serene.

In 86, our dwelling embraced both joy and despair.

Forever etching in memory, a tale we now share.

A Letter to Autumn

Who in this century

Holds onto paper and pen stubbornly

To write a letter to autumn?

Other than the enchanting words of fairies in fairy tales,

Apart from proud emojis closing their eyes in ecstasy,

Texting is a lot cozier.

A second's speed will reach your go through the labor of a season,

To write a letter to autumn with a watercolor mood.

In the late autumn's brilliance, a symphony unfolds,

Embraced in the bosom of sunlight's golden glow.

The whispers of light frost dance upon the earth,

Creating an orange ambiance, a tapestry of fallen leaves' worth.

A color is faintly traceless, like the breath of clouds in tranquil flight.

A hue holds the secrets of the heart, burning with fervor bright.

Autumn's ethereal missive gently descends,

Bestowed upon the waltzing leaves,

Presented to the pristine moonbeam,

Nestled in the chronicles of time,

Transmuted into a reverie's kaleidoscope butterfly.

May every chilly autumn hue serenely navigate the deluge of rain.

May all yearnings dwell within celestial groves, veiled in the mists of time.

Sunlight & Plateau

Embraced by Sunlight on the Plateau,

Golden rays dance in fervent delight,

Cool winds whisper tales of grace.

A shallow stream, and a lake fading from sight,

Become a solemn song hidden in the heart of the grassy sea.

A touch of gold, a warmth too bright,

Wrinkles the made-up faces,

Unveiling the city's pretense and apathy.

Please hold an umbrella made of clouds, with stars peeking
through.

Time lingers in the breath I take.

Clouds caress tear-stained eyes anew,

Fingers point to winds that my soul awakes.

The wind's gentle touch caresses my essence,

Guiding my heart along a path divine.

The grassland, an original and final sanctuary for open presence,

Rejects the chill of a cold gaze from the moon.

In the cradle of the grassland, where spirits roam free,

Infinite journeys last against freedom's gentle breeze.

Allow me to rest here for a thousand years,

Filtering the sunlight through a pure white *Khada*.

With pen tip poised, I wait in the wind,

Until a blade of grass sprouts from my feet,

Two or three snow lotus blooms adorn my brow.

In the Whispering Wind

As the wind stirs, a wanderer crosses the ethereal ferry,

Blending the seen with the unseen,

Drifting through the depths of my soul serene.

I am the wilderness, the essence of time embraced by the moon's

wild climb,

A fleeting dream standing strong in the wind's dance.

In the whispering breeze,

Snow lotus blooms in divine song.

And faith's wings take flight.

In the whispering wind, a romance weaves its tale.

A sanctuary found in the bird's harmonious wail rises to heavens

vast and bright,

Pursuing the fire's celestial light.

Ever-warming my moistened perspective.

Oh, gentle breeze, the eternal guide,

Nurtures blossoming petals with pride.

Oh, wind is golden fragrance of a natural temple.

Oh, wind unravels the entombed deceit.

Oh, wind is a solitary holy being on the precipice of time.

When will you whisk me away to the shores?

Where stars gleam bright?

Chinese Culture

I gaze upon the ancient land with deep emotions.

That's the cradle of life, where our ancestors rest peacefully.

Vast plains accommodate rebels and the tenacious poplar trees.

Lonely mist over the river, the poplar trees pay their respects.

Culture nurtures me like milk, fostering my strength,

Embracing forgiveness in mistakes, illuminating the soul.

The Chinese genes run strong, coursing through our blood.

Four mythical creatures guard the directions, belief enduring.

The eight trigrams swirl, unveiling cosmic mysteries.

In the *Classic of Mountains and Seas*, myths abound.

Rivers flowing, Tian Shan mountains vast,

Atop Kunlun's peak, poetic sentiments soar.

Oracle bones inscribed with *Qiang* characters,

Great Yu's legacy and the *Book of Songs* enshrine time.

The enduring *Classic of Lacquer* is immortal,

As poetry in Tang and Song Dynasty, opera in Yuan Dynasty.

Smoke signals rising between the borders of Qin Dynasty and Song Dynasty,

Agriculture's origins are deeply rooted in the first rice.

Yellow Emperor's Canon of Medicine and *Compendium of Materia Medica* sing the song of the ecosystem.

Zodiac signs and solar terms mark an eternal cycle.

Five thousand years of culture, six thousand years of civilization,

Have refined elegant gentlemen, an ocean of wisdom.

Spring Festival reunites billions of people.

Qingming Festival and Ghost Festival deepen people's sentiments.

Dragon boats racing, the fragrance of artemisia and calamus, new grains of rice,

Intangible cultural heritage shine brightly, with porcelain and *Khada* whispering blessing.

The Yin ruins, *Sanxingdui* Museum are stars shining in the East.

Poetry and wine of *Li Bai & Su Shi* exude passions.

Over nine million six hundred thousand square kilometers, dialects resonate,

Calling out to China with deep affection.

Fifty-six ethnic groups are tightly knit pomegranate seeds,

Inheriting dreams, forging magnificence together.

Bone Flute

Which ancient hunter was it who ruthlessly clipped your wings?

Feathers of dread scattered in echoes.

Recalling that solitary sky,

White bones, scorched by the blazing sun,

Gaze softly towards the snow-covered mountains.

Bones are transformed into a flute,

A blend of icy steel and fiery flame.

A stubborn bone is destined to be pierced by fate.

Sufferings in the world fill the depth of the hole.

The eagle's stance is an unshakable curse.

Its spirit mirrors the waning ancient sun.

The flute rests silently by the dry lips of the flute player,

Whose teeth half-open and half-closed, unable to be restrained.

Melodic notes, caught between wakefulness and slumber,

Bring forth the revival of treachery.

Beast fur, pungent odors, and raspy roars gush out of the valley-like bone flute...

Oh, flutist, the symbols you unknowingly unveil

Awaken the ancient, mythical tale

A heart hollowed, empty, and frail.

As he follows the mysterious, white stones,

Icy rivers prevail,

Witnessing the ice hoarded and fire's fierce gale by man and
beast...

Oh, the relentless piper,
Why do you transform into a bird tonight,
Pecking at my blurred vision?
A tale sends shivers down my soul.
I can't resist crying out in anguish.

Shocking Tragedy: The Blue Diexi

In the winter of 2003, I journeyed to Diexi in Mao County, Where I was met by a heavy snowfall, covering the rocks and foliage, rendering the landscape bleak, yet hauntingly beautiful. As I visited the Earthquake Museum, I learned that at 15:50:30 on August 25, 1933 , Diexi was struck by a powerful 7.5-magnitude earthquake. Overwhelmed, I composed this poem.

In my dreams, I often witness flashes of lightning,
As the mountains collapse, the earth splits,
And the fierce winds wail in surreal twists.
The ancient city, once standing proudly, now crumbles in silence.
A frozen wave seals the anguished cries of countless souls in despair.

Under the starry night, the moon's gentle plea goes unheard.
Falling stars, with muted whispers, lament in the depths of the sea.
The ethereal spirit of dreams adorns a patched cloak,
Leading me through secret tunnels of enigmatic time.
I shall engrave the pathway home deep within my soul,
Revealing to the relentless yearning the delayed tidings of hope.
Bestow upon the most resplendent bride a gown pristine in the city of *Qiang*,
And grace the groom's swift steed with fresh, verdant greens.

The silver-haired sage, unburdened, basks in the sunset's glow,

While sprightly children, nurtured, flourish and grow.

Dreams, I beseech you, guide these vibrant souls with care,

Grant every precious life a calculated escape.

Oh, fervent host, withhold the cup that cleanses me.

Your countenance radiates a smile of eternal bliss.

The bridal garb, is adorned by the bride's skilled hand.

A tapestry is woven with yearning and auspicious echoes.

Do the elder's eyes, reaching to the celestial dome,

Perceive the ethereal bird, no longer in this sky to roam?

Where do the deities, revered by the devout, reside?

Do they not offer hints, or prophetic signs to confide?

A feast of a hundred and sixty tables lasts from morn till noon.

The union of two esteemed lineages stir laughter and blessings.

Within the cacophony of joy and well-wishing cries,

The potent liquor of the barley, yet again, amplifies.

Thunders from all sides echo beneath the earth,

Where souls of bliss and sorrow reside.

Cast away all mundane matters from your view,

Ascend with me upon the final voyage of Yu the Great[2].

Oh, enigmatic ghost,

---

[2] Yu the Great, also known as Da Yu, is an important figure in ancient Chinese mythology and history. He is considered to be one of the earliest recorded rulers in Chinese history and is renowned for his skills in flood control.

Why does my voice betray its once faithful guise?

Within these hollowed halls, why do my words go amiss?

And why does my brush, on parchment, languish and die?

My tear-filled eyes, like stars in splendor, weep,

As my fingers caress the gentle sunlight's touch.

But the sunlight, speechless, and I awash in woe.

Before time entombs the grandeur,

For seventy years, a vigil is kept by remnants,

Amidst the ruins where desolation sears.

Before the time tunnel seals

Which mountain outmatches the rest?

Which river's rush none can rival in its zeal?

Golden towers spin in quake's thrall.

Fault lines grind and fracture, appalling.

Each second strains, with horrified appeal.

Sliding ladders drag all innocent beings

To dark abyss of hell in an instant reaching.

Wanderers adrift at edge of yearning's call,

Forever dwelling in past's old mud,

Beneath the waters, in memories' thrall.

On a cascade of effervescent bubbles,

My soaked wings are unable to mask the agony deep within.

Life's end is a fate we cannot withstand.

In the tranquil passage of your timeless years,

Loneliness is an innate inheritance of human nature.

As splendor and ruin fade together, who becomes whose sentinel?

Life is but a fleeting traveller in the employ of time.

Descendants clutch fragments of wonder, civilization's tears.

When I stand still by the tranquil shore where ink meets sea,

My thoughts, like strings, ebb and flow perpetually.

The icy gleam propels the cyclical chains of the seasons,

Whose soul can withstand the serenity of desireless seasons?

The forest of thoughts, though deep and grand,

Struggles against the clandestine fire beneath the land.

If happiness is thus defined,

People hold fate's tape unconfined,

Allowing life to fade in its own time unwind.

The yearning soul with dreams paradise combined,

Our footsteps light in afterlife will find.

The grief of quakes stands as the oracle of time and judgement.

Diexi, forever submerged, becomes an eternal enigma.

The lush valley, teeming with greenery, is unmasked by modernity.

A thousand leagues of cerulean waves are perfect for the hermit's tranquility.

The time slips away from your own corporeal form.

The ancient road's horse hooves are a distant memory in a silent storm...

I gaze upon the heaven,

No figures, no snow-capped peaks, a hidden presence within.

60

Blind Eyes

The left eye was once blazed with fire, the right with a spring.

The blossom is for you, the crescent a bowstring.

The quiet night of a winding life remains silent,

As *Er Quan Ying Yue*[3] gently steps over the azure sky.

In the night's shroud and daylight's veil,

The icy peak of life gleams with a mystical tale.

Ancient prayer flags dance, symbols of peace,

In the dark pupils, a smile is as tender as the breeze.

Bestow upon me sixty seconds of celestial splendor,

To fathom the rose for which green leaves tender,

With what ardor and grace it abides,

In love's enduring embrace that never subsides.

Once, I glimpsed the spectral ghost of yesteryear.

She floatcd lightly past the sparks of the vanishing fireworks.

Her defiant spirit tethered to the echoes of memories had gone,

Whisper not to her of the enigma of my eternal fate.

A cosmic dance of gold, wood, water, fire and earth intertwined.

My heart's devotion treads a path through time,

Where mud and thorns become a tapestry woven in its stride.

---

[3] also known as *Two Springs Reflecting the Moon*, is a famous piece of traditional Chinese music. It is a pipa and guzheng duet that was composed by the renowned musician and composer Liu Tianhua in the early 20th century.

Emotions are unseen by mortal eyes.

I reach for joy with verse, sensing the verdant breeze,

Whispering and swelling through canyons of contemplation.

Who was the creator of pioneering Braille,

Allowing my fingers to learn how to read?

I sense this world with my palms,

That lean back to back with the frail shoulders.

Desires of this life are so tilted that they incline into

The forever desolate smoke of the vast desert.

In the braille's undulating universe,

Whose eyes meet innocent voices in the dark?

Whose heart leads the climb up azure peaks?

In a city of solitude and desolation,

Which light illuminates fragile souls?

Whose love steers the grand river of life?

To Future Phantom

I am uncertain

If with thoughts boundless in their flight,

You might in this poetry tome abide

For a century or a millennium.

In which season will you, future soul,

Untap my musings like aged wine?

Do the post-biological beings

Capture the ghosts of wisdom's passed

In a quest to preserve their ethereal essence?

Tonight, soft moonlight curves as a silken thread.

Who will embed the chip of my memory in the heartwood of a
tree,

In the breeze's embrace, amidst the tree's shadow, in the realm of
dreams?

Poised in a golden dance, I stand within a dreamlike garden.

Will there be friends who know there, in serenity?

When I become a tree that blossoms with thought,

Might he be the regal blue peony, reaching skyward?

As my branches spread wide like the wings of a roc,

Can these ancient wings call forth wind, rain, and thunder?

Plucking the strings of an ancient zither with tender care,

Inquiring if the mountains still rise with majesty rare,

I send to you the moonlight and breezes of a bygone century,

And play seven-stringed lyre in tones crisp and merry.

How many verdant fields remain, where life's bounties abide?

In the heart of the moon, does a haven for humankind reside?

Warmth and solace forever in shadow abide.

In this world woven of memory and dreams,we glide.

Do the rivers flow crystal-clear, untouched by time's swift tide?

As generations unfold like petals in time's embrace,

Will the child of my child's child find solace in my grace?

Unaware that the tree's gentle nod is an echo of ancestry,

A playful spirit from eons past smiles through the leaves.

Child of my lineage, have you brought home tea anew,

From Qingcheng's slopes, where mist kisses the dew?

Let's boil the water, steep the leaves in a fragrant cup,

And brew a pot, so that fragrance weaves its song,

Awakening senses that slumbered for so long.

Together we'll sip as tea leaves unfurl,

In a timeless dance with the world's gentle swirl.

May this moment of connection, hearts with warmth, banish all
fears.

Upon unlocking the electronic family lineage,

We unveil a saga of perpetual pilgrimage,

Caressing the timeworn place names with tender care,

Where wishes flourish like rays of sunlight fair.

Let your heartbeat gently embrace stillness,

Slow the rhythm of a beating heart,

And gently sip from an ancient tome.

In the beams of thought, solitude's seeds scatter

Upon the soil of tomorrow,

In anticipation of a tender hand to nurture.

In the future, you are but a mystery to me,

Just as I am a stranger to the future's gaze.

Within the ethereal glow of time, where shall we find our place?

Do not partake in the solitude's wine, let it burn alone,

Abstain from coffee without milk to guard our hearts from the
shadowed depths of the inner demon.

After sifting through countless streams filtered a hundred times
over,

It shall dilute the visage of blood types.

Who shall sip from my bittersweet elixir?

Behold the tumultuous upheaval of ancient mountain birth,

As the mirage of yesteryear's market slumbers in repose.

And tonight's stars fail to illuminate the former beauty within me
of poetry.

How many sorrowed hearts curl tight among the world's vast
volumes of poetry?

Oh, future self, set free the ethereal butterflies,

Turn my poetry into a vibrant realm of animation,

Where a hidden river flows, leading to both past.

A Day to Dream Away

Childhood's innocent mirth fades,

Like whispers of wind carrying fallen leaves,

As glorious fairy tales yield to worldly shades.

Life's battleground is inundated with relentless aims.

A tapestry of dazzling thorns is spun by cravings.

Time dances in a cyclical, fleeting notion,

From one dungeon to the next, a brittle commotion.

In the hustle, in the rush, life stays ablaze,

A symphony of moments, a mesmerizing phase.

On a tranquil day, let's simply dream,

Free from all the material, concept, and scheme.

No need for socializing or chasing of any kind,

Just costless, consumptive, and thoughtful unwind.

Temporarily abandon all promises and the blind,

In a placeless day, let's breathe with peace of mind.

Borrow from the sky a feather, to unravel desires within,

Cast off all masks cruel, let true beauty begin.

Even the rocking chair yearns for sunlight's embrace,

And green grass weeps in solemn, gentle grace.

When fate greets you in narrow dreams with a fearful sigh,

The awakening void becomes the cure for wandering eye.

Return to the realm of ice and mist, as waters flow,

In a daze, fold your hands, let the weary soul rest in snow.

Lay me to rest as the network's dawn breaks,

Where the sea gazes at the sky's silent ache.

Let snowflakes chase the ice at frozen grace,

And the seeds of spring dream in winter's embrace.

Through the tunnel of Qingming, to eternity's gate,

I am a flower bud lost in the cosmic estate.

Youthful fruits on branches are swaying in morning's embrace.

Should the day arrive when my shadow leads the breeze,

Do not bury me in cold, damp soil's hold,

Lest I decay with fallen trees, lost in darkness untold,

Nor in flames that may engulf my restless plea,

And not in waters deep, where dreams endlessly roam free.

Bury me in the cyber grave, my kin.

I'll carry away a blue rose within,

And withered love is attuned.

I'll lean on the scent of almond wine,

Rereading ancient poetry, singing long laments,

Through the translucent rain of the web, pure and refined.

Eyes like cold light, piercing the dawn of desire,

The wild fireflies transform into silver stars,

Polishing my melancholic brow afar.

A Man's War

Spear and shields, cold gazes afar.

Inevitably, we lie together in a warehouse.

Ice meets fire, as conflict and luxury,

Prove each other's worth, in this delicate tease.

Darkness and dawn in a dance, entwined,

Imprisoned within your form, where shadows unwind.

A flicker of flame is a touch of icy memory,

And careless whispers, like arrows, take wing.

No one is dispensable in this intricate dance,

Piercing the tender, the fragile, the deep,

Awakening wounds that we silently keep.

Just a wisp of fire can cause sensitivities to sting.

The flames of war outside life's domain,

Scorch the very essence within.

Only the soul howls through the night,

Afraid to enter one's own empty city,

Allowing the tiger to return to the mountain as an excuse.

Torrential rain washes away the world's worries.

The lightning of the spirit strikes oneself.

Caged bats cover the sky,

Sending out electric waves in every corner of the body.

How I wish to be a bottle of fine wine,

Breaking free from the constraints of the bottle,

And flowing through your veins.

The war of a man seals the destiny of the soul.

The war of a man licks its own wounds.

I banish the lure of darkness.

My righteousness is also my wickedness.

In the sea of suffering, I struggle for the joy of life.

The changing of the stars signals the dawn.

The result of the final battle is both separation and reunion.

Reason determines the ultimate fate of the hero.

The Final Orchid on the Table

Not a single orchid shall,

In years, transform to Jade-like fossil.

She would simply be one extinct species in botany's tome,

A tragically scented allure of a bygone area.

As the forlorn soil fills the parched pot,

My pen tip is a wounded bird.

With an indelible sentiment,

I insert a sapphire-blue plume,

To freely yearn at my desk.

Wild Cotton in the Sun

Wild cotton,

A stretch of white cascades into my sight,

Quietly crystallizes on brittle branches.

This year's wild cotton has turned into a bittersweet longing.

Next spring, I'll scoop a dear spring to soak the errors of time.

In winter's embrace, vibrant life hoards fragile warmth.

When fierce winds sweep down the hillside, wild cotton,

Are you cold?

Who shall shield you from the chill?

Do you face the sun,

Wrapping your blooms around the watching boughs?

Oh, wild cotton, how long have you graced this slope?

In biting winds, you await a gaze from afar.

Self-reflection seeks a sacred space,

Expanding desires stab with aching sharpness.

As radiant sunlight weaves through your stamen,

The crystalline snow tenderly wafts your gaze.

Will distant memories hum languid tune?

I yearn to harvest your smile, cloud-like and bright,

Beneath a drifting snow's embrace, a soft pillow still awaits.

Do all fruits bear the weight of pearl-like tears?

Is the fragrant snow of summer's heart rolling in?

With a thousand wild cotton blooms as my gentle repose,

No more will nightmares chase me through the night.

With a thousand wild cotton blossoms cradling my dreams,

I shall nightly envision your smile, radiant as the sun.

Time of Words

In the vast expanse of time's canvas,

Dreams in hues so vivid they ascend.

On the hands of ages, silent whispers

Echo in the autumn breeze, moonlit tend.

Many ancient tomes now bear the weight of years.

Pages yellowed, edges frayed, secrets they keep in silent tears.

Chinese characters, playful sprites, bring laughter to my eyes,

Each stroke a genealogy, a tale of the East's ancient sighs.

Sometimes I despise words' deceitful play.

A vibrant poppy is hidden deep within my heart's domain.

My weary soul seeks solace in dreams' array.

I witness nameless souls adrift, their freedom restrained,

Awaiting redemption on foreign ships, confined in disarray.

The elusive purple light and lightning snatch me away.

I traverse the river of time with stealth, a wanderer lost in rhyme.

Residing within the DNA of the East,

Each strikes a character's prime.

With precision, square by square, they dance on the stage of calligraphy,

Swaying through the ages, from seal to cursive, each script's legacy.

Words, a love-hate relationship, are my heart's opiate embrace,

Weaving my soul with threads of spectral spirits in dreams so surreal.

Nameless souls voyage on ships to distant shores, their purple glow a beacon,

Capturing me in their ethereal dance, their light forever an enchanting.

From dusk to dawn, I inhale the essence of words,

Weaving them into poetry.

Wings of joy and sorrow carry the faith's ascent,

Each stroke flighting a verse.

Words dictate the fates,

Breathing their solitary existence, a song of their own.

From first word to final character,

A maple leaf falls from the sky,

Words too deep for ink.

Floating in the current of life, its message whispered to the wind.

A testament to a life lived is entwined with the trials of words, till the end.

The Little Wooden Puppet

Breathing in the ancient scent of wood,

The puppet of a small stature resides,

In the riverbed of my dreamland.

With the moon's rustless light as backdrop, it abides.

A gaze of a lifetime is pure and serene.

I search for a seed to bloom as a tree.

Its branch guiding my heart,

I journey through life's ebb and flow.

You, the wood grain etched with time's touch,

Rest deep within the eyes of the ages.

I, a bird on a branch, yearn for sunlight's clutch.

In the boundless sky, our spirits engage.

I seek you in the spring of the previous life,

In the chill of autumn's present life.

In myriad ways, your essence I trace.

My heart wanders in love's enchanting chase.

An oath in the winter of lives yet to be,

Shields from illusions and sorrow's stain.

Embracing a single flame, wild and free,

We chant a song of yearning in the radiant domain.

In the realm where sunlight dances and shines,

Together, we soar through boundless skies divine.

Mending a Tattered Note

A weary one-penny note, frayed and torn,

Nestled in a noble leather pouch.

Whispers of woes wore a creased facade,

And a heart battered and forlorn.

I mend the torn note,

Which bears the weight of solemnity.

I witness farmers toiling under the scorching sun,

Their perspiration crystallizing into precious gems.

They till the earth through seasons as a lifetime spun,

Clutching the harvest in their calloused hands,

For salt and warm quilts spun.

We care for aged parents, life's final sands,

While cherubic faces demand to be fed.

With a flawless sheet of ivory paper,

Mending a torn note

Is regaining a memory from a decade past.

In 1980, when I was but a child of ten,

A family of five striving to make ends meet,

Was enveloped in the hum of my mother's sewing machine.

My father, a printer, returned home late.

The sharp scent of machine oil filled my childhood diary;

My sisters and I enchanted by graceful dolls in a shop window.

Sighing in wistful symphonies,

Mother handed us pennies with her generous hand.

We could purchase two chilling treats on a scorching day.

A mere piece of ordinary paper currency

Bears the weight of life's highs and lows.

Filled with purpose and meaning,

Each note grants weary souls a peaceful repose.

A vast sum of money screaming and yelling,

The soaring stocks hold its attention compelling.

A small, wounded note quietly tells

The profound essence of labor's devout.

My Eternal Lover: The Nib

Ice folds unfurl to dancing butterflies,

Flitting on invisible wings;

Through verdant dreams they fly.

Oh nib, at times you stray too far,

Even my blood dances to your call.

In the liminal space between reality and dream,

You elegantly bid me farewell in the closest way.

In this season,

I often forget the enchanting spell of spring.

It's your embrace, pure as stars,

That gilds my melancholic brow.

On the canvas of reality,

Swirls a tapestry of smiling scenery.

Rain breaks, tender feelings reborn because of you.

Poetry in My Palm

Within the fragrant fold of my palm,

A single invisible bloom takes hold.

No green leaves or fruits to show,

It stands slim and graceful in its glow.

At the doorstep of the season's embrace,

Exudes a Sandalwood-scented grace.

Ebbing and flowing with the moon's gentle sway,

On a night the tides dance and play.

In the palm that people say I clench so tight,

Lies a brush of ancient might.

Splattering ink with spirited might,

Paints the night lotus, clear and bright.

Blooming just once in a starlit guise,

The lotus illuminates the depths of thoughtful skies.

My poetry, in the airy season's sigh,

Is a delicate spark that catches the eye.

Blooming within the heart of those who dull,

It will never be mediocre, nor servile.

Passing by

I glide beyond the looking glass,

Where my reflection forgets my face.

Through the whispering winds I pass,

As they weave tales of my grace.

Over the mountain's silent peak,

The clouds' tales fade away,

Through the river of time's mystique.

In the words' waters, I find my way.

Bathed in the golden sunlight's glow,

I enjoy the scent of May and songs of July.

I tread through your thread-bound books,

Where bookmarks of crimson leaves lie.

In the echo of your hurried steps,

I hear the ancient hooves gallop past.

Through the memories your heart still keeps,

Where the flames of vengeance last.

Time is the unanchored ship of fate,

Where life's sorrows are not forever bound.

Whether embracing brilliance or confronting the mundane state,

We joyfully pass through, yet fly away into oblivion.

At times, we flow like water's graceful dance;

At times, we remain silent as a slumbering volcano.

Beyond the ethereal, the river of the universe,

Stands the pinnacle scaled by the luminous light of thought.